Cannon used during the battle is on display at the
Colonial National Park in Yorktown, Virginia.

An 1896 drawing of the British surrender at Yorktown

Cornerstones of Freedom

The Story of
THE SURRENDER AT YORKTOWN

By Zachary Kent

CHILDRENS PRESS ®

CHICAGO

Midnight and Cornwallis is taken!!

Library of Congress Cataloging-in-Publication Data

Kent, Zachary.

   The story of the surrender at Yorktown / by Zachary Kent.
     p. cm. — (Cornerstones of freedom)
   Summary: Recounts the last military campaign of the
Revolutionary War which culminated in the surrender of Cornwallis'
men to the French and Americans in 1781.
   ISBN 0-516-04723-X
   1. Yorktown (Va.) — History — Siege, 1781 — Juvenile
literature. [1. Yorktown (Va.) — History — Siege,
1781. 2. United States — History — Revolution, 1775-
1783.] I. Title. II. Series.
E241.Y6K47 1989   89-33784
973.3'37 — dc20   CIP
                                         AC

PHOTO CREDITS

Copyright © 1989 by Childrens Press®, Inc.
All rights reserved. Published simultaneously in Canada.
Printed in the United States of America.
   2 3 4 5 6 7 8 9 10 R 98 97 96 95 94 93 92 91 90

Clattering horse hooves echoed through the brick streets of Philadelphia, Pennsylvania, in the early morning blackness of October 24, 1781. After a four-day journey, Lieutenant Colonel Tench Tilghman galloped into the colonial city carrying a stunning message from his commander, General George Washington. Searching through the darkened streets, Colonel Tilghman stopped beside a startled old German night watchman. He asked directions to the home of Thomas McKean, president of the Continental Congress. Within minutes the exhausted officer hammered his fist upon McKean's door. Once inside, he presented McKean with Washington's thrilling news. "Sir: I have the Honor to inform Congress," the note exclaimed, "that a Reduction of the British Army under the Command of Lord Cornwallis is most happily effected. . . ."

As he continued along his late-night rounds, the old German watchman excitedly rang his handbell and shouted: "Past three o'clock and Cornwallis is taken! Past three o'clock and Cornwallis is taken!" Soon the bell in the tower of the state house — Independence Hall — also pealed in noisy celebration. By daybreak everyone for miles around had learned of the victory at Yorktown. Patriotic citizens yelled and danced in the streets. The surrender of the British in that small Virginia town surely meant the United States had won the Revolutionary War.

The bloody fight for American independence had begun six long years before. Since the 1600s Great Britain's kings and queens had ruled the settlers in the thirteen colonies. In the 1770s, however, the British Parliament decided to raise needed money by taxing certain trade goods. Forced to pay import taxes on such items as glass, paper, and tea, Americans from Massachusetts to Georgia loudly grumbled about their rights. Many complained that King George III gave them no vote in Parliament. At town meetings angry colonists chanted, "No taxation without representation!"

The argument exploded into war on April 19, 1775. In the Massachusetts towns of Lexington and Concord, colonial militiamen clashed with red-coated British soldiers. As the American Revolution began in earnest, radical patriots like John Adams and Patrick Henry more loudly than ever demanded freedom. The thirteen colonies sent representatives to Philadelphia to discuss the issue. On July 4, 1776, the ringing of the Liberty Bell in the Pennsylvania state house told excited citizens that the members of the Second Continental Congress had signed a Declaration of Independence.

Von Steuben and Washington greet Lafayette.

To command the Continental Army the Congress chose forty-three-year-old George Washington of Virginia. With uncommon energy, stubbornness, and leadership, Washington held his army together through the next difficult years. The American fight for liberty excited some European noblemen. The youthful Marie du Motier, Marquis de Lafayette, sailed from France to offer his services. From Prussia came Friedrich Baron von Steuben, a tough drillmaster who helped whip Washington's troops into military shape. Although battered and defeated in several battles with their British enemies, the Continental army refused to give up.

American troops at Valley Forge

Winter encampments proved worse than the battles. In crude log cabins the poorly supplied rebels huddled through the bitter, freezing weather. Dr. Albigence Waldo accurately described those first cruel days at Valley Forge, Pennsylvania, in 1777. "Poor food—hard lodging—cold weather—fatigue—nasty clothes—nasty cookery...smoke and cold, hunger and filthiness. A pox on my bad luck." General Washington walked among his starving, sickly men and later wrote, "I feel...for them and from my soul pity those miseries which it is neither in my power to relieve or prevent."

In April 1778 officers rushed through the camp shouting happy news. The government of France

Benedict Arnold   Sir Henry Clinton

had recognized the independence of the colonies and soon would join the war as an ally. With renewed hope, the bedraggled Continental army vowed to keep on fighting. The trials of the next two years required every ounce of their revolutionary spirit. While the British army of Sir Henry Clinton rested in comfort in New York City, Washington's hungry soldiers suffered in small watchful camps to the north and west.

In May 1780 the British captured the city of Charleston, South Carolina, and began terrorizing the southern countryside. In September, Washington discovered that one of his favorite generals, Benedict Arnold, was a traitor. Only quick action prevented Arnold from surrendering the fort at West Point, New York, to the British. In spite of every setback, Washington clung to hope.

Uniform of a French soldier (above). General Washington meeting Count Rochambeau, head of the French army (right)

Suddenly in the summer of 1781, the American general saw a chance for final victory. A French army of some 5,000 men had landed earlier at Newport, Rhode Island. Washington persuaded its commander, Count Jean-Baptiste de Rochambeau, to march south and join forces with the Continentals. Well-equipped and wearing handsome uniforms trimmed with bright regimental colors of red, blue, yellow, and pink, the French army smartly marched into the American camp at White Plains, New York, on July 6. The Americans greeted the French with wild cheers. The ragged condition of the rebel troops shocked many French officers, however. "I cannot insist too strongly how I was surprised by the American army," wrote Count de Bourg. "It is truly incredible that troops almost naked, poorly paid, and composed of old men and children and Negroes should behave so well on the march and under fire."

Eagerly Washington made plans to destroy the British army in New York City. Daily he awaited news of the arrival of Admiral François Count de Grasse's French fleet, which he hoped would blockade New York harbor. In August, though, Admiral de Grasse sent word he intended to sail to Virginia's Chesapeake Bay. Angrily Washington later wrote, "I was obliged . . . to give up all idea of attacking New York." Instead he snatched at the opportunity presented by the French naval movement. From Virginia General Lafayette reported that an army of 7,500 men commanded by General Charles Earl Cornwallis was encamping at the coastal town of Yorktown. If he raced southward, perhaps Washington could surprise and destroy this powerful British army.

Leaving 3,500 troops behind to guard New York, Washington ordered the march to begin on August 25. By swinging some regiments toward New York's Staten Island, he fooled General Clinton into thinking he still planned to attack New York City. At the last moment these troops turned west and hurried across New Jersey. Too late Clinton realized Washington's true intent. Beneath the hot summer sun the allied army of 2,500 Americans and 5,000 French marched. Bands played patriotic songs as the troops tramped along the dusty roads. Ox-drawn wagons rumbled behind, carrying supplies as well as boats and pontoons for river crossings. Citizens of Philadelphia crowded the streets and cheered the army as it paraded through that city.

Washington rode ahead while General Rochambeau and other French officers chose to sail down the Delaware River by boat. Near Chester, Pennsylvania, a messenger from the south brought splendid news. The French fleet had arrived in Chesapeake Bay. His escape route by sea blocked, surely Cornwallis was trapped. "I never saw a man more thoroughly and openly delighted than was General Washington at this moment," remarked the Duke de Lauzen. "A child whose every wish had been granted could not have revealed a livelier emotion," agreed the Count William Deux-Ponts. When General Rochambeau's boat reached Chester, the normally calm and dignified Washington was excitedly waiting to tell him the news. "I caught sight of General Washington," recalled Rochambeau with some surprise, "waving his hat at me with . . . gestures of the greatest joy."

Nothing remained but to hurry the army to Virginia. Leaving his faithful officers to perform this task, Washington galloped ahead. On September 9 he rode up the winding drive leading to Mount Vernon. For the first time since the start of the war, 6½ years earlier, Washington visited his home overlooking the Potomac River. Even among his family, however, the general was unable to relax. Pushing onward, he reached Williamsburg, Virginia, five days later. With open arms General Lafayette gladly welcomed Washington into his camp. Already Admiral de Grasse had landed 3,000 fresh French troops, swelling the size of the allied army in Virginia. That night Washington learned that De Grasse's fleet of twenty-four ships successfully had fought off the attack of a nineteen-ship British force. With that crucial victory, De Grasse announced he would stay and blockade the mouth of Chesapeake Bay until the end of October.

Washington and Rochambeau study the British fortifications.

Certainly Cornwallis seemed doomed now. "We have got him handsomely in a pudding bag," gleefully declared American General George Weedon. Urgently Washington wrote to General Benjamin Lincoln, "Every day we now lose is comparatively an age. . . . Hurry on then, my Dear Gen'l, with your Troops on the wing of Speed." On September 26 the last of the soldiers finally marched into the Williamsburg camp. Two days later, Washington's French-American army, numbering more than 16,000 men, started on the last eleven miles to Yorktown. "We prepared to move down and pay our old acquaintance, the British at Yorktown, a visit," happily exclaimed one American veteran, Sergeant Joseph P. Martin.

In the autumn sunshine of September 29, Washington on horseback examined the open ground leading to the little coastal trading town. The British had abandoned their outermost defenses. Closer to town, however, many obstacles remained. Small forts called redoubts ringed the village, guarded by rows of sharpened logs. Redcoat soldiers had dug trenches in the sandy soil, and half a mile across the York River they defended the small town of Gloucester, too. Immediately, Washington ordered most of his troops into the abandoned British earthworks. He hurried the remainder north to block escape from Gloucester.

Through the next days the Americans and French swung picks and shoveled dirt as they improved their position. Even British cannon fire failed to interrupt their work. One cannonball plunged into the ground where Washington and other officers were standing. A shower of sand rained down on the men, including a startled army chaplain. As the fellow examined his spattered hat, Washington smiled and remarked, "Mr. Evans, you'd better carry that home and show it to your wife and children."

Washington decided to take Yorktown by siege, drawing his artillery closer and closer to the town until Cornwallis was pounded into surrender. On the rainy night of October 6, therefore, one thousand volunteers crept forward to within 800 yards of the British lines. With their shovels and picks they furiously dug into the soil. By dawn British sentries cried out in alarm. Washington's volunteers had built a new line of trenches within easy cannon range. Piling dirt in front, the Americans and French next built gun emplacements. With sweat and muscle they dragged their heavy artillery pieces into place.

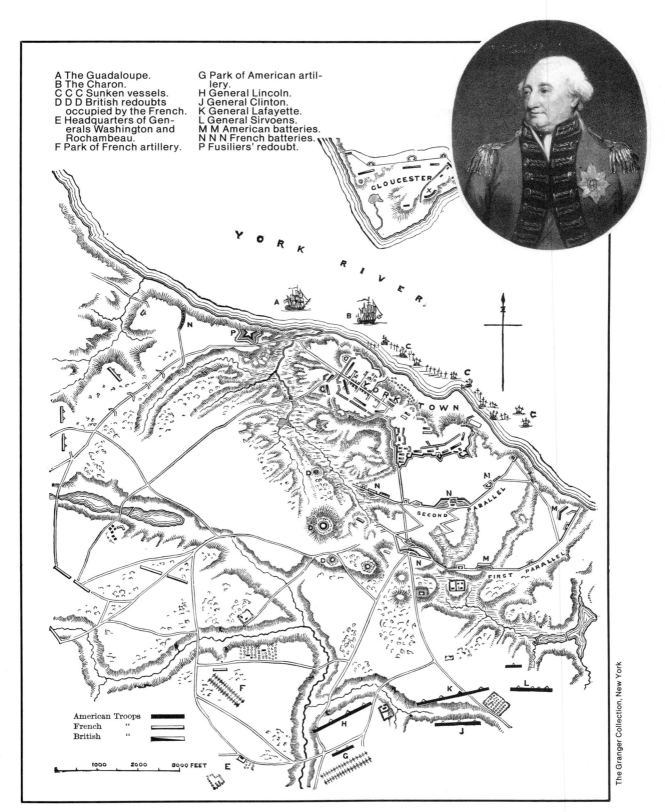

A The Guadaloupe.
B The Charon.
C C C Sunken vessels.
D D D British redoubts occupied by the French.
E Headquarters of Generals Washington and Rochambeau.
F Park of French artillery.
G Park of American artillery.
H General Lincoln.
J General Clinton.
K General Lafayette.
L General Sirvoens.
M M American batteries.
N N N French batteries.
P Fusiliers' redoubt.

American Troops
French   "
British   "

1000   2000   3000 FEET

General Cornwallis and the map of the Yorktown battlefield

This painting by Howard Pyle shows George Washington firing the first gun at the siege of Yorktown.

At three o'clock on October 9 French cannon fire on the far left started shelling Yorktown. Two hours later Washington himself fired the first American gun. His twenty-four-pound cannonball whistled through the air. By some reports, it crashed into a house, smashed across a dinner table, and killed a British general. Through the night the artillery rained destruction down on Yorktown. "The fire continued incessant from heavy cannon and from mortars and howitzers," reported the stunned Cornwallis, "... until all our guns on the left were silenced, our work much damaged, and our loss of men considerable."

Shocked Yorktown citizens fled to the beach and dug protective caves in the sandy cliffs. Rumors reached Washington that even Cornwallis and his staff had "burrowed" shelters in the ground. Daylight on October 10 showed the awful damage of the bombardment. Many Yorktown houses sagged and smoldered. Proudly General Lafayette turned to Virginia Governor Thomas Nelson, Jr., who was visiting the allied lines. "Is there some spot in the town we should hit?" he asked. Governor Nelson instantly pointed to a fine tall house. "Cornwallis may be there. Have them fire there. It's my house." When the gunners hesitated, Nelson patriotically offered a reward to the first man to score a hit. Soon cannonballs arched through the sky and slammed through the brick walls of the Nelson house.

The Nelson house was hit by cannonballs fired from American guns.

By October 11 fifty-two allied guns were firing into Yorktown. Pennsylvania militiaman Dr. James Thacher soon wrote, "I have more than once witnessed fragments of mangled bodies and limbs of British soldiers thrown into the air by the bursting of our shells." Part of the British army consisted of German troops called Hessians. These mercenary soldiers fought for King George III in exchange for money. Cowering now near the beach, Hessian Private Johann Doehla claimed the shelling "felt like the shocks of an earthquake." Loads of hot shot soon set a British ship in Yorktown harbor ablaze, filling the sky with flame and smoke. Under the steady bombardment, the British defenses weakened.

To tighten his grip on the enemy, Washington ordered the digging of a second parallel trench on the night of October 11. In the darkness, brave work parties moved to within 400 yards of the British lines. Every man carried "a shovel, spade or grubbing hoe," remembered Lieutenant William Feltman. As the British sent shells screaming overhead, the soldiers dug. By morning their ditch stretched 750 yards. Measuring roughly 3½ feet deep and 7 feet wide, it provided the advancing allies with ample protection. During the following two days the French and American artillerymen wrestled

George Washington inspects the French artillerymen in the trenches.

additional cannons into this new forward position.

Washington's second parallel remained incomplete on the right because two British forts—Redoubts Numbers 9 and 10—stood in the way. On October 14 Washington ordered night attacks to capture the two forts. A French assault force was to take Redoubt Number 9. Closer to the York River, Lieutenant Colonel Alexander Hamilton won the assignment of leading 400 American soldiers against Redoubt Number 10, also called the Rock Redoubt.

Soon after dark the attackers silently swarmed across the open ground. Prepared to chop through the sharpened logs that ringed the redoubts, some men carried axes. Others hauled ladders with which to climb the high dirt "parapet" walls. To insure complete surprise, most of the Americans carried unloaded muskets, relying on their bayonets to do their bloody work. "I know you'll be brave men," whispered Rhode Island militia Captain Stephen Olney. "If you lose your gun, don't fall back—take the gun of the first man killed." Pressing forward, the axmen soon encountered the bristling wooden barriers. Suddenly an alert sentry within the redoubt called out a challenge. An instant later the British defenders fired a musket volley that lit up the night.

"At this our men broke silence . . . ," recalled Captain Olney. The Americans roared battle cries as the axmen hacked at the sharp logs before them. "Rush on boys! The fort's our own!" shouted the officers. Surging ahead, the soldiers crawled and twisted through the sharp wooden logs. They scrambled across deep craters left by allied mortar shells and soon they were climbing up the redoubt's walls.

Musket balls whizzed through the air and scream-

Both sides fought fiercely.

ing men clutched at wounds. Reaching the top of the parapet, the Americans fiercely lunged with their bayonets. Frightened and outnumbered, the small garrison of Redoubt Number 10 surrendered within minutes. Soon afterward, shouts of victory revealed the French troops' success at Redoubt Number 9.

The swift and violent fight cost the allies about 120 dead and wounded. But it sealed the fate of the

British. From these redoubts Washington could now fire artillery into every corner of the town. In Yorktown, Lord Cornwallis scribbled a message to General Clinton. "My situation now becomes very critical. We dare not show a gun to their old batteries, and I expect their new ones will open To-Morrow Morning." Though he had hoped to receive reinforcements from New York, now Cornwallis realized how useless even they would be.

As his defenses crumbled, British honor required some show of resistance. In the blackness of early morning on October 16, therefore, some 350 picked British troops grimly attacked an unfinished section of the second parallel. Thrusting savagely with their bayonets, the redcoats drove off dozens of shocked French soldiers. After spiking several cannons so they would not fire, the raiders then retreated back to Yorktown.

The attack hardly slowed the allied bombardment. Through the day French and American guns still roared. Crouching in the Yorktown trenches, Hessian Corporal Stephan Popp remarked that the crashing shells made it seem "as though the heavens would split." Johann Doehla exclaimed, "Everybody easily saw that we could not hold out much longer in this place. . . ."

Desperately Cornwallis made one last effort to save his army. On the night of October 16 the British gathered every boat still floating in Yorktown's harbor. Cornwallis planned to ferry his men secretly across the York River to Gloucester. With luck he could then smash through the encircled allied troops to the north and retreat all the way to New York. Under cover of darkness one wave of troops succeeded in crossing but a sudden drenching rain and violent windstorm made additional crossings impossible. Soaked and shivering, the British and Germans staggered back ashore. Lord Cornwallis realized his last gamble had failed.

At sunrise on October 17 one hundred allied cannons opened fire at close range, showering still more exploding shells down on Yorktown. Shortly after nine o'clock a small figure climbed high upon the foremost of the battered British defense works. Standing alone, this drummer boy vigorously beat a steady roll. "Had we not seen . . . the redcoat when he first mounted," American lieutenant Ebenezer Denny later declared, "he might have beat till doomsday. The constant firing was too much for the sound of a single drum; but when the firing ceased, I thought I had never heard a drum equal to it—the most delightful music to us all." Everyone understood the appearance of the brave young boy. His

The surrender terms were negotiated at the Augustine Moore house (below) and delivered to George Washington (opposite page).

special drumbeat signaled the British desire for a conference.

As the allied guns fell silent, a British officer waving a white handkerchief walked toward the American lines. Soon his important message was delivered into Washington's hands. Cornwallis wished to "settle terms for . . . surrender." Ordering a halt to fighting, Washington named two peace commissioners to arrange final surrender terms.

On October 18 Colonel John Laurens and the Vicomte de Noailles (Lafayette's brother-in-law) met with two British officers at the home of Augustine Moore, behind the allied lines. The men haggled over surrender details until late into the night. Presented with the written articles at eleven o'clock the next morning, George Washington quietly signed them and ordered an aide to add the line:

"Done in the trenches before Yorktown in Virginia, October 19, 1781."

News of the stunning British defeat quickly spread through the countryside. In the pleasant, bright weather of the early afternoon, an enormous crowd of Virginians moved toward Yorktown in wagons and carriages to witness the historic surrender ceremony. For a mile along the main road leading out of the town the allied army formed two lines. On the right the French in their handsome white linen uniforms stood in military splendor. On the left, although in tattered uniforms and sometimes barefoot, the Americans arranged themselves with even greater pride. After years of hardship and sacrifice, this was their day of final triumph.

In silence the victors waited. At last at two o'clock the British advanced from their ruined battlements. With shouldered muskets and flags cased, the column slowly marched as their bands played a mournful tune called "The World Turned Upside Down." Many of the redcoats angrily scowled, still unwilling to believe they had been defeated by an army of ragged rebels. One New Jersey militiaman noted that the British officers in general "behaved like boys who had been whipped at school. Some bit their lips; some pouted; others cried."

The British surrendered on October 19, 1781.

Bitterly embarrassed by his defeat, Lord Cornwallis failed to appear at the head of his troops. Instead he sent his second-in-command, Brigadier General Charles O'Hara, to represent him. As he neared the waiting allies, O'Hara spurred his horse toward General Rochambeau. Clearly he wished to surrender to the French rather than the Americans. Rochambeau, however, shook his head and pointed

British General Charles O'Hara presents his sword to General Lincoln.

to Washington across the road. Swallowing his pride, O'Hara rode to the Continental commander in chief. With cool formality, Washington refused to accept O'Hara's sword. He waved him aside to his own second-in-command, General Lincoln. Lincoln had been shamed by the British during his surrender of Charleston, South Carolina, the previous year. Now by a satisfying twist of fate Cornwallis's army was to be officially surrendered to him.

General Lincoln directed the British into a nearby field known ever afterward as Surrender Field. The defeated soldiers reluctantly marched forward inside a circle of waiting French cavalrymen. "Ground arms!" a sergeant barked as rank upon rank of British and Hessians sullenly tossed their weapons into piles. Then they marched back to Yorktown, prisoners of war.

Within hours Lieutenant Colonel Tench Tilghman was riding north to Philadelphia with the spectacular news. The once powerful army of General Cornwallis had ceased to exist. That night the American soldiers at Yorktown celebrated as never before. One observer declared, "The officers and soldiers could scarcely talk for laughing; and they could scarcely walk for jumping, and dancing and singing as they went about." These hardy veterans knew the British could not recover from their terrific loss. Great Britain would stall another two years before finally granting American independence in 1783. But in truth the war had just ended with the sound of fifes and drums outside that little Virginia town. Surely the surrender at Yorktown marked a day the world turned upside down. Against the greatest possible odds the United States of America had won its right to liberty.

Dressed in military uniforms, volunteers reenact the battle at Yorktown.

INDEX

About the Author

Zachary Kent grew up in Little Falls, New Jersey, and received an English degree from St. Lawrence University. Following college he worked at a New York City literary agency for two years and then launched his writing career. To support himself while writing, he has worked as a taxi driver, a shipping clerk, and a house painter. Mr. Kent has had a lifelong interest in American history. Studying the U.S. presidents was his childhood hobby. His collection of presidential items includes books, pictures, and games, as well as several autographed letters.